The photo on the cover
March 10, 2016 at the
Orchid show. The flow
Dad had of giving my Mom and his three daughters, an orchid corsage for Easter each year when I was growing up. Thanks, Dad for your thoughtfulness.

NATURE SPEAKS

CONTENTS

SPRING

1. Abundance

2. Responding

3. Spring's Loss

4. Our Homes, 1942 to 1965

5. Simplicity

6. Rebirth, This Spring

7. Attachment

SUMMER

8. Twitty's Struggle

9. Flying Flames

10. Painted by the Light

11. Color

12. Keeping Safe

13. Patient Struggle

14. Gleeful Sounds

15. Presence

16. Back to Summer

17. Fly Away

18. Storm Responses

FALL

19. Listen

20. Nature Boy

21. Monday, Winter Coming

22. Crossing

23. Autumn Glory

WINTER

24. Heavenly Beards

25. Silvery Winter

26. Sunday at Hilton Head

27. Sea Pines Beach

28. Hazy River

29. Sad

30. Bleak Winter

31. Then, Now, Tomorrow

SPRING

Photo taken by Mary Pat Henehan from "March for Our Lives" Spring 2018

Abundance

Pink spring flower
rebirths for Mother's Day.

Feathery petals
touched by the
Divine Artist
dabbing a bit
of red on its tips.

A bright scent
ascends
calling,
rest your nose
in the center.

Losing count
of the petals
awe at the beauty.

Blessed by Mother Nature.

Storm Responses

Thunder, lightning
scary.

Remember, umbrella
inconvenient.

Man heads for a tree,
he's killed on the golf course.

Grandma Charles
prays for the right kind of rain.

Tomato plants
drink the moisture.

Parsley, sage
grow an inch.

Birds delight
in puddles.

No umbrellas.

Spring's Loss

At the border, cries of children
ripped from their parents' arms.
No spin can justify this reality.

Where is our moral compass?
The needle is stuck.

I have never seen anything like this.
Revulsion and trauma spreads like lightning
across the nation.

Vital bonds broken by cruel bias
responsibility calls me to speak out.

Our Homes, 1942 to 1960, Dover and Pratt

Hostas along our neighbor's fence
Her cats sneaking around the leaves.

Marigolds edge our daisies
purple irises with smells of lemon,
yellow tulips, and red roses.

Lily-of-the-valley, anoint the ground
with their sweet spring scent,
Great Grandpa Inwood smiles.

Pink and white phlox in front of the
garden swing set
framed by hanging willows.

Auntie Mary Jane helps,
ready the summer playground.

Space to swing and kick off shoes
the farthest shoe
wins.

Simplicity

Sipping morning coffee

a robin, singing in the rain
a wake-me-up song,
perching on the rim of my patio potato pot

no raincoat, no boots
enjoying each drop

doesn't jump at the
roar of thunder

undisturbed.

Rebirth, This Spring

Bright tulips
red, white, pink
born in the sunlight.

Daffodils
show off
their golden brightness.

Cardinals
sing
a wake-up tune.

Rose bush
leaves
emerge.

Herb garden,
chives
up six inches.

"March for
our lives"
organizing growth.

Women
want positive
change.

All creation
crying out
"Never Again."

Gun policy changes
in the air,
bloodshed in the schools.

Getting our attention once again, we ask
how do we protect our children,
as they grow?

Dedicated to Mary Kay Meagher on her birthday today.

Attachment

We usually see
Brown Thrashers toward the
woodline.

Undulating flight pattern,
almost like a butterfly stroke
in the air.

Shy birds,
but close to the house
this year.

Knitting needle-like
beaks,
to grab their
earth lunch.

The yew close to the back window
is their new home.
Launching from the wheelbarrow handle,
they plop onto the nest.

Eggs must be sturdy
to handle the sudden
weight upon them.

Awaiting the birth,
we ask ourselves
what will baby
Thrashers look like?

The birds know all this.
We look forward to
being taught.

SUMMER

Photo by Mary Pat Henehan from vacation, Door County, August 2018

Twitty's Struggle

Adorable little one on
the road where we were walking.

Frozen in place.
mother bird squawking.

We could not get the little bird off the road
Twitty's claws clamped the asphalt.

Such a helpless feeling
wishing for someone to tell us how to help.

A prayer is what came to mind:
"Courage."

And this poem to remember Twitty's short
but moving life.

Flying Flames

Starting my yoga practice
in *Savasana.*

A flash of gold, at the corner of my eye
What is darting through the sky?

Gulls at sunset.

Painted by the Light

Sun peeks out of the lake.

I experience gold on my legs,
arms, neck, face.

This must be what enlightenment feels like.

Color

Surprise in the sky
orange is the new August moon.

You are supposed to be white,
brightness shimmering on the lake.

Why orange tonight
making the lake sparkle?

Some can't take the bright glare of white.
Tangerine is mellow, tastier, diverse.

The world needs calming.
Thank you.

Keeping Safe

Two sisters holding hands,
cross the street.

Big sister protecting
little sister,
warms my heart.

Time passes,
years and miles apart,
how does our
love look as we navigate life?

Inner connection,
confidence,
strong bonds,
Will invisible family ties cut across time?

Patient Struggle

Prednisone, you are a miracle worker
with side effects.

His red blood cells working again
though you are a mischief maker:
Insomnia, irritability, aggression.

Glad to see steroid dosage decrease
60, 50, 40, 30, 20, 10 mg.

Only to return to 40, 20 mg
with more side effects
we descend again.

Hoping to see you disappear
leaving his hands steady again,
shaking gone.

Looking forward to seeing him symptom free
I await this with joy.

Bye, bye my medicine friend or foe,
complexities of healing.

Gleeful Sounds

Joyful squealing from the baby pool
showers sprouting and falling like a water umbrella.

As the 2-, 3-, 4-year-olds jump into the spray,
screams of delight.

Too long since I have heard such glee
music to my ears.

The memory marching through
my day, my week; I yearn for more sounds like these.

Presence

Sitting at the edge of the Mississippi River

movement of water calms the mind,

carrying worries away.

Arriving in the present moment

I feel the cleansing, the lifting of burdens.

Is now all that matters,

all I really have?

Back to Summer
(Senior State Games June 2018)

Keeping legs limber in the hotel pool after getting gold in pickle ball.

Push off for the backstroke, rotate hips, visualizing winning tomorrow's race.

I have a chance to set the record for the Individual Medley for my age group.

Can swimming be a life long skill? Can I reach these goals?

Memories of summers at Edgewater Country Club pool,

recalling a favorite white bathing suit with a yellow cummerbund,

lazy summer days, knitting Argyle socks for my boyfriend

between refreshing swims and back dives off the board.

Watching out for my brothers and sisters, no big deal.

They are entertained in the pool.

I recall how relaxed I was at sixteen,

apart of me wishes for that feeling back.

Fly Away

Bonnie collects white-dotted leaves
of Milkweed.

Brings them
into her home,
as she tries to save them.

Feeds fresh milkweed leaves
to the new born caterpillars,
protecting them from birds,
a special netted house.

She watches with
Buddha-like concentration,
as the pupa form before her eyes.

Finally, the Monarchs emerge
wings are dry, and begin
their 2,500-mile journey.

Bonnie sings a blessing song
sending them on their way.

Dedicated to Bonnie Mitchell

Storm Responses

Thunder, lightning
scary.

Remember, umbrella
inconvenient.

Man heads for a tree,
killed on the golf course.

Grandma Charles
prays for the right kind of rain.

Tomato plants
drink the moisture.

Parsley, sage
grow an inch.

Birds delight
in puddles.

No umbrellas.

FALL

Photo taken by Mary Pat Henehan at Pere Marquette Park, 2017

Listen

Early morning hoot
stops me in my tracks, as I pick up the paper.

Where is the call coming from?
The oak in our neighbor's lawn?

Lovely, mystical sounds, moving into my heart.
Is it a Great Horned Owl;
the Great Spirit?

A huge wing flashes through
our Sweet Gum tree
responding with another toned call,
lovers finding each other.

How did they find each other so quickly?

Nature Boy

Attending thirsty tomato plants,
out of the corner of my eye
I see a six-year-old, two doors down,
dancing naked in his yard.

When did a child taking off his clothes
to run in the yard
become abnormal?

"I was naked so I hid myself"
but God replied to Adam:
"Who told you, you were naked?"

This young boy had not been told,
he was not constrained.

He awakened my inner six year old.

Monday, Winter Coming

New week, energy from the Sabbath.
Movie "Victoria and Abdul" inspired me.
Saw the power of a friendship.

Exercise group,
snack outside
checking phone less.

Smoothie snack, break of fruits and veggies.
Get to some of those tasks I put off.

Lunch with hubby,
love shared.

Cut off the dead parts of the plants,
in you go for the winter.

Progress made on paperwork,
practiced music for next event.

Register for "Creating Moments of Joy"
prepare materials for teaching.

Preparing dinner,
love the aroma of saffron
the mixtures of Paella.

Cubs have to win tonight,
wash during commercials,
communicate with family and friends.

Songs from "The Voice" fill the house.
we love watching the mentoring by the coaches.
Such talent encouraging.

Can our days be poetry?

Crossing

Driving north on Price
heavy traffic going south passed by,
as I approached John Burrough's campus.
Out pops a buck
a prince crossing the street
elegant antlers held high.
What a contrast, all the engines pushing forward,
a handsome deer walks with pride.
I watched, no family following, then drove on.
Deer are homeless too.
Has their food sources become more challenging?
Nature is resilient.
Surprises can appear anywhere.

Strong Seasons

Resting head and back on
autumn sunset maple.
Strength comes to bones.

My glance drawn upward
shades of red and gold
celebrating this season.

Blasts of beauty
leading to the mystery
of leaving.

Gentle scars.
Simplicity
in naked branches.

Cold, damp, dark
nights of winter coming.
Bare, vulnerable you.

What is your strength?
To sway gracefully
in winter's cold and not break?

Blossoms coming
death and life
connecting.

WINTER

Photo by Mary Pat Henehan, Wreathe Display at the Missouri Botanical Gardens, Dec. 2018

Heavenly Beards

Riding my bike
on a path
lined with live oak trees,
pointed fingers of hanging moss.

Curly, a perm by nature?
Silver threads
knitting my day together.

So much awaits us
in creation,
if we open our eyes.

See the earth,
be glad,
take it all in,
today is all I have.

Silvery Winter

Silver, a color, a metal rich with meaning
Comforting the eye, a silvery moon.

Silver is peaceful, precious,
time, encased in silver.

The polish of years reflected in silvery gray strands.
Silver bells bring joy.

Listen to silver, sterling and pure.
Clear notes, silver tones.

Silver says elegance, nobility.
Silver medals reward service.

Silver is strength yet common,
used in everyday living.

Scissors, pins, needles, spoons, forks, knives,
mirrors, stars, flutes.

Silver, a beatitude.
rich in giving,
eternal.

Silver is Sr. Mary William Sullivan.

Sunday at Hilton Head

Five sun bathing turtles
on stones in the canal by our path,
speaking to me without words
relax, enjoy the warmth.

Lunch at Red Fish
crab, lobster, shrimp roll
satisfied my hunger.

Celebrated with peppermint ice cream
rolled up in a chocolate
covered cake.

Afternoon walk
three deer staring at us and we at them
followed by Big Blue doing
Tai Chi walking in the lagoon.

Light, I pray to the week ahead.

Sea Pines Beach

Riding my bike by Palmetto trees
with their woven trunks.

Sound of crashing waves
relieving my stress.

Soothing smell of salt in the air,
Dolphins, following me on my ride.

Changing shades of blue sky
cotton ball clouds.

Cocker spaniel, running freely,
happy to be released from its travel cage.

Ears flapping, excitement of movement
running in and out of the ocean.

Letting go of
life's challenges.

Taking in sun rays,
vacation, a life saver.

Hazy River

Eagles
out of sight.
Mist hovers over
the waters.

Reminds me of
a Monet painting.

Boaters ignore
the fog.

Blinds to
the side of the Mississippi
hunters left the lingering smell of gunfire.

Country blinded by
confusion,
gun control
debate stuck.

Gray sky today,
space to await clarity,
blue skys again.

Can acceptance of
foggy events in life
be the key to happiness?

Driving home,
eagles appear once more.

Sad

President boasts
a military parade,
tanks destroying the streets.

Dreamers' voices
not being heard,
demeaned by some politicians.

Murder of
Esmond Bradley Martin,
for protecting Kenya's wild animals.

Global warming
coral reefs destroyed,
glaciers melting.

Federal funds cutoff
from community clinics
mothers and babies go unserved.

Who will undo this
mindless cruelty?
You, me, my grandniece Julia?

When will change happen?

Bleak Winter

Neosho,
what are you doing?

Third graders
Asked to sell
Raffle tickets.

For what?
An AR 15
Semiautomatic gun.

Evil or stupid?
Regard for children
has disappeared.

Adults made this decision?
Can we call them adults?
Or robots
of our gun culture?

Listen to the Voices ringing out
from Parkland Students
"We are not safe."

Then, Now, Tomorrow

Then

>Learning ice skating
>Chase Park, Chicago.
>Practicing skating backward
>in backyard rink.

>Learning footwork for figure eights,
>the warming house was the best part
>of Touhy Beach Rink.

>Sledding down
>Mr. Walter's hilly front lawn
>on Dover Street.

>Toboggan sledding
>with Dad and sibs
>in Cook County Forest Preserve.

>Snowman,
>with snow packed firmly,
>scarf and hat secured.

>Curling rink,
>sweep the ice in front of the stone,
>causing it to go faster toward the bull's eye.

Now

Careful to get the paper
from the driveway, walking on the lawn
to keep from falling on the ice.

Shoveling snow, chipping the ice,
clearing the walkway.

Faithfully attending my circuit training group on
Mondays and Wednesdays.

Writing and bringing poems and chapters
to our Weekly Writing Group.

Playing indoor pickle ball when I can,
getting ready for Golden Games in April.

Planning for spring garden,
potatoes, tomatoes, beets, parsley and sage.

Organizing a grief support group
at the Newman Center at Washington University each
semester.

Tomorrow

I will do my 15th Indoor Mini Triathlon.
Good training for Nationals, swimming and pickle ball tournament,
this June.

Hoping to publish my poems this year. Meeting with Apple
Creatives to look at self-publishing process.

Examining new communication methods, Twitter, and Instagram.
Refreshing a graduate course for 2020,
transitioning from Blackboard to Canvass.

Attending Family Reunion in Connecticut,
Lou and Fran's September, October Weddings.

Planning a 30th wedding anniversary trip to Australia and
New Zealand with my husband.

What will future years bring? I hope to balance fun times
of then, with the nows of winter, and the hopes for
tomorrow.

Acknowledgments:

Jack Renard, my husband for his patience and listening to poems as they were being created.

Theresa Mancuso for publishing "Listen" in Affinities, April, 2019.

My Writing Group: Charles Gallagher, J. Terry Gates, Judith Kelvin Miller, Karen A. Palmer, Robert A. Saigh, Cheryl White, Steve Robbins, Diane Bleyerd, Mort Levy, Deni Dickler, Elaine Payne, Dan Weinberg.

Poetry Teacher: Kim Lozano

Made in the USA
Columbia, SC
17 September 2019